THE DONKEY'S TALE

A Christmas Musical

Text by Herbert Chappell and Tracey Lloyd
Music by Herbert Chappell

Kevin Mayhew

We hope you enjoy the music in this book. Further copies are available from your local music shop or Christian bookshop.

In case of difficulty, please contact the publisher direct by writing to:

The Sales Department
KEVIN MAYHEW LTD
Rattlesden
Bury St Edmunds
Suffolk
IP30 0SZ

Phone 01449 737978
Fax 01449 737834

Please ask for our complete catalogue of outstanding Church Music.

First published in Great Britain in 1997 by Kevin Mayhew Ltd.

ISBN 1 84003 039 9
ISMN M 57004 104 6
Catalogue No: 1400152

0 1 2 3 4 5 6 7 8 9

Front cover illustration by Andrew Geeson
Cover design by Jaquetta Sergeant

Music Editor: Donald Thomson
Music setting by Daniel Kelly

Printed and bound in Great Britain

Contents

About the Composer

HERBERT CHAPPELL has been composing since he was a choirboy at Bristol Cathedral. His first major success, *Daniel Jazz*, led to a number of other works for young musicians. In addition to compositions for the concert hall, such as his highly acclaimed *'Caribbean' Concerto* for guitar, he has composed more than two hundred scores for films and television. These range from music for BBC serials and the plays of Shakespeare to the musical *James and the Giant Peach*, the opera of *The Importance of Being Earnest* and such favourites of young children the world over as *Paddington Bear* and *Huxley Pig*. As a leading producer and director of television films he has created many successful classical music programmes – the original Rome concert of The Three Tenors, Andrew Lloyd Webber's *Tell me on a Sunday* and programmes with André Previn, Kiri Te Kanawa, Leonard Bernstein and many other eminent musicians.

THE DONKEY'S TALE

Text: Tracey Lloyd and Herbert Chappell
Music: Herbert Chappell

1. NO ROOM AT THE INN

Outside the stable a great crowd of animals put up a sign which says: 'No Vacancies!'

13
dogs and cats and smel - ly cam - els. Miaou! Baa! Neigh! Moo! Miaou! Baa! Neigh! Moo!
gliss.
15
16
hand-claps
No va - can - cies! Full up in - side! No va-can-cies!
19
sim.
Full up in-side! No va - can - cies! Full up in - side! There's no
23
room! There's no room! There's no room! There's no room at the

27
inn! The smell is e-nough to dis-gust
30
us. Ev-'ry-one packed to the door.
33
Blame it on Cae-sar Au-gus-tus! We got no room for a-ny more
36
cows and hor-ses, sheep and goats and dogs and cats and smel-ly ca-mels.

38
Miaou! Baa! Neigh! Moo! Miaou! Baa! Neigh! Moo! No va-can-cies!
gliss. 15
41
hand-claps
sim.
Full up in-side! No va-can-cies! Full up in-side!
44
Half of the Animals
No va-can-cies! Full up in - side! There's no room! There's no
48
room! There's no room! There's no room! There's no room! There's no room! There's no
Remainder of the Animals
There's no room! There's no room! There's no

53
room! There's no room at the inn!
room! There's no room at the inn!
ff
57
Bull
A
mp staccato
59
bull al - ways gets what he asks for. And
8va sempre
61
this is - n't my kind of joint. So

63
get off my corns or I'll sharp - en my horns, and I'm
8va sempre
65
sure you will all get my point!
67 Horse
Hor - ses are fond of their com - forts. This is
8va sempre
69
not what I'm used to at all.

71
How can you sleep with a ca - mel and a sheep, and a
8va sempre
73
All Animals
large smel - ly heap of man - ure? Man -
75
ure. Man - ure.
8va sempre
77
Mary and Joseph arrive, leading their donkey
Innkeeper
Sor - ry, we're full to the raf -
loco

79
- ters. There's real - ly no room to - day. Per -
mp
82
slower
haps we've got room in our sta - ble. You can snug - gle up warm in the hay.
dolce
p
85
All Animals
ff a tempo
No va - can - cies! Full up in - side!
hand-claps
ff subito
88
No va - can - cies! Full up in - side! No va - can - cies!
sim.

91
Half of the Animals
Full up in - side! There's no room! There's no room! There's no
95
room! There's no room! There's no room! There's no room! There's no
Remainder of the Animals
There's no room! There's no room! There's no
99
Very slow
ff
room! There's no room at the inn.
ff
room! There's no room at the inn.

2. THE DONKEY'S SONG

The Donkey does a little dance
and addresses the other animals

Tempo di Soft Shoe Shuffle (♩. = c.96)

19
feet are sore. Clip-pe-ty, clip-pe-ty, clip-pe-ty, clip-pe-ty,
23
clop. Hee - haw! Hav-ing come all this way find-ing
26
no-where to stay but a sta - ble, seems a pi-ty.
29
We've had a snub in e-ve-ry pub in Roy - al Da-vid's Ci-ty. C -

33
lip. C - lop. C - lip - py, clip - py, clip - py, clop.
37
The Donkey performs a tap dance
The Donkey strikes a balletic pose
Clip - pe - ty, clip - pe - ty, clip - pe - ty, clip - pe - ty, clop. Hee - haw!
40
All
(♩ =100)
Yeah!
mp
sim.
44
Donkey
1. I have a job in a car - pen - ter's shop, a
2. How, you may ask, do I find my - self here?
3. All ga - ther round and I'll tell you my tale be -

49
nice and qui - et life. Re - gu - lar
wea - ry, sad and worn? Miles from my
fore we hit the hay, Jo - seph, my
54
hours and re - gu - lar pay. Plen - ty of oats and
home and co - sy bed? Puf - fing and blow - ing and
boss, is kind and proud, Ma - ry, a hum - ble
59
plen - ty of hay. None of your troub - le and
darn near dead. Foot - sore and for -
girl who vowed to be his bride one
63
rall.
strife. None of your troub - le and
lorn. Foot - sore and for -
day. to be his bride one
rall.

67
slower
strife. When a rude a - wake - ning
lorn. Just when I should be
day. Ma - ry is blessed by the
slower
70
came to me as I walked a - long the dust - y road to
pen - sioned off, Start - ing to feel the strain. Here I am in a
Lord on high, an an - gel from a - bove told her she'd have a
74
After verses 1 & 2
allargando
5
D.S.
Ga - li - lee, sing - ing my plain - tive song. C -
crum - my old pub, sing - ing a sad re - frain.
ba - by boy
allargando
D.S.
78
After verse 3
tenuto
Ma - ry's heart was filled with joy, prai - sing God for the gift of Je - sus, the King of
Attacca

3. MAGNIFICAT

12
Lord and my spi - rit, my spi - rit, my
15
spi - rit hath re - joiced, re - joiced, re -
18
joiced in God, my Sa - viour. For
21
he, for he, for he hath re - gar - ded the

25
low - li-ness, the low - li-ness of his hand - mai - den for be -
29
hold, be - hold, from hence - forth
33
all ge - ne - ra - tions, all ge - ne - ra - tions, all ge - ne - ra - tions shall
36
All mp
call me bles - sed, bles - sed,

40
div.
bles - - sed.
44
Mary
For he that is migh - ty hath mag - ni - fi - ed
pp
48
me and ho - ly, ho - ly, ho - ly is his
52
name. And his mer - cy is on them that fear

56
All
him, that fear him, that fear him through - out
59
cresc
all ge - ne - ra - tions.
Più mosso
f
He hath shew - ed strength with his
63
arm.
He hath scat - tered the proud in the im - a - gi -

67
na - tion of their hearts. He hath put down the
na - tion of their hearts. He hath put down the
71
migh - ty from their seat and hath ex - alt - ed the
migh - ty from their seat and hath ex - alt - ed the
75
hum - ble and meek. He hath filled the hun - gry with
hum - ble and meek. He hath filled the hun - gry with

79
good things and the rich he hath sent
good things and the rich he hath sent
83
emp - ty a - way. He, re - mem - ber-ing his mer - cy, hath
emp - ty a - way. He, re - mem - ber-ing his mer - cy, hath
86
hol - pen his ser - vant Is - ra - el. As he pro-mised to our
hol - pen his ser - vant Is - ra - el. As he pro-mised to our

90
fore - fa - ther Ab - ra - ham and his seed for
fore - fa - ther Ab - ra - ham and his seed.
93
e - ver, for e - ver.
f
Glo - ry, glo - ry, glo - ry be to the
96
Glo - ry to the Fa - ther, glo - ry, glo - ry,
Fath - er. Glo - ry, glo - ry,

99
and to the Son, As it was in the be-
and to the Holy Ghost. As it was in the be-
102
gin-ning, is now and e-ver shall be,
gin-ning, is now and e-ver shall be, e-ver shall
105
world with-out end, world with-out end, world with-out end,
be, world with-out end, world with-out end, world with-out

108
A - men, A - men,
end, A - men, A -
112
allargando
A - men, A - men.
- men, A - men, A - men.
allargando

4. JOURNEY TO BETHLEHEM

17
rall.
but he said: 'Thy will be
rall.
21
(♩. = ♩)
done.'
sim.
And
25
so they re - turned to the car - pen - ter's shop where
29
they were to make their home. But

33
Ma - ry had hard - ly set - tled down when, in
37
e - ve - ry vil - lage and e - ve - ry town, there
41
came a com - mand from Rome, there
45
came a com - mand from Rome:

Slower
Roman Soldier
Cae-sar is go-ing to tax you all for e-ve-ry pen-ny you're worth, and
ev-'ry-bo-dy must re-turn at once back to your place of
rall.
rall.
birth.
Donkey: 'Come on everybody, all together...'
All (♩. = c.96) (Roman Soldier exits)
C - lip. C - lop. C - lip-pe-ty, clip-pe-ty
clop. Clip-pe-ty, clip-pe-ty clop. Hee - haw!
legato

66
I've got a back - ache and my feet are sore.
70
Clip-pe-ty, clip-pe-ty, clip-pe-ty clip-pe-ty, clop. Hee - haw! Hav-ing
74
come all this way find-ing no-where to stay but a sta - ble, seems a
77
pi-ty. We've had a snub in e-ve-ry pub in Roy - al Da -vid's

81
Ci - ty. C - lip. C - lop. C - lip - py, clip - py, clip - py,
85
The Donkey performs a tap dance
clop. Clip - pe - ty, clip - pe - ty, clip - pe - ty, clip - pe - ty, clop. Hee - haw!
The Donkey strikes a balletic pose
89
All
Yeah!
(♩ = 100)
mp
sim.
Donkey
So
94
that's how we got here in Beth - le - hem with no - where to

99
lay our heads. That's our sto - ry as
104
far as it goes. What hap-pens next? Well, no - bo - dy
109
knows, but now it's time for bed,
114
rall.
now it's time for bed.
rall.
Attacca

5. LULLABY

Gentle waltz tempo
pp
5
Animals
(Dozing off) Baa!
9
Baa! Hee! Haw! Baa! Baa! Hee! Haw! Baa!

* *Sing this page through once in the normal way then several times as a round with each new voice starting at points* A *to* D.

6. SONG OF THE ANGELS

The Animals sleep. Angels appear to the shepherds.

The shepherds start to wake up
a tempo
Slower
8
mp
pp
cresc
fff
And on earth, peace, good-will to all.
And on earth, peace, good-will to all.
And on earth, peace, good-will to all.
f
12
Shepherds
f
We can hard - ly be-lieve our eyes,
dim.
15
sit - ting here, guard-ing our sheep, hud-dled from the snow in the

18
fire - light glow, try - ing not to sleep, when sud - den - ly:
21
All
Wake up! I think I see an an - gel. Wake up! There's
24
an - gels up on high! Wake up! No need to be fright - ened.
27
Shepherds
Fol - low the gold - en star through the win - try sky.
cresc.

30
All
And a mes - sage the an - gels bring
33
tells us all mar - vel - lous things. Je - sus born this
36
ve - ry morn, he's the King of kings. So all of you
39
f
wake up! I think I see an an - gel. Wake up! There's
f

42
an - gels up on high!
Wake up!
No need to be fright - ened.
45
Fol - low the gold - en star through the win - try sky.
48
ff marcato
fp
Come with us,
Hur - ry to the sta - ble,
51
Hur - ry, hur - ry, hur - ry to the in - fant King,
fp
Come with us,

54
tell-ing ev'-ry stran-ger all a-bout this won-der-ful thing, for sud-den-ly the
57
sky is a-live with wings and the an-gels ho-ver,
mf
60
sing-ing their song, tell-ing us all a-bout a child so small,
63
born to right each wrong, so all of you wake up! I
f

66
think I see an an - gel. Wake up! There's an-gels up on high!
69
Wake up! no need to be fright - ened. Fol-low the gold - en
72
star. Fol-low the gold - en star through the win - try
75
1st Shepherd
sky. I
8

77
1st Shepherd
sub. pp
had a fun-ny dream. We must be see-ing
2nd Shepherd
So did I. We must be see-ing
3rd Shepherd
So did I. We must be see-ing
8
sub. pp
82
pic-tures in the fire. I had a fun-ny dream.
pic-tures in the fire. So did
pic-tures in the fire.
8

87
I thought I heard an an - gel -
I. I thought I heard an an - gel -
So did I. I thought I heard an an - gel -
8

93
choir. I had a fun - ny
choir.
choir.
8
pp

98
dream.
I'm not ex - act - ly cer - tain where I
So did I.
I'm not ex - act - ly cer - tain where I
So did I.
I'm not ex - act - ly cer - tain where I
8
103
am.
So let's be on our way.
am.
On our way.
am.
On our
8

108
We'll take him a new - born
We'll take him a new - born
way. We'll take him a new - born
8

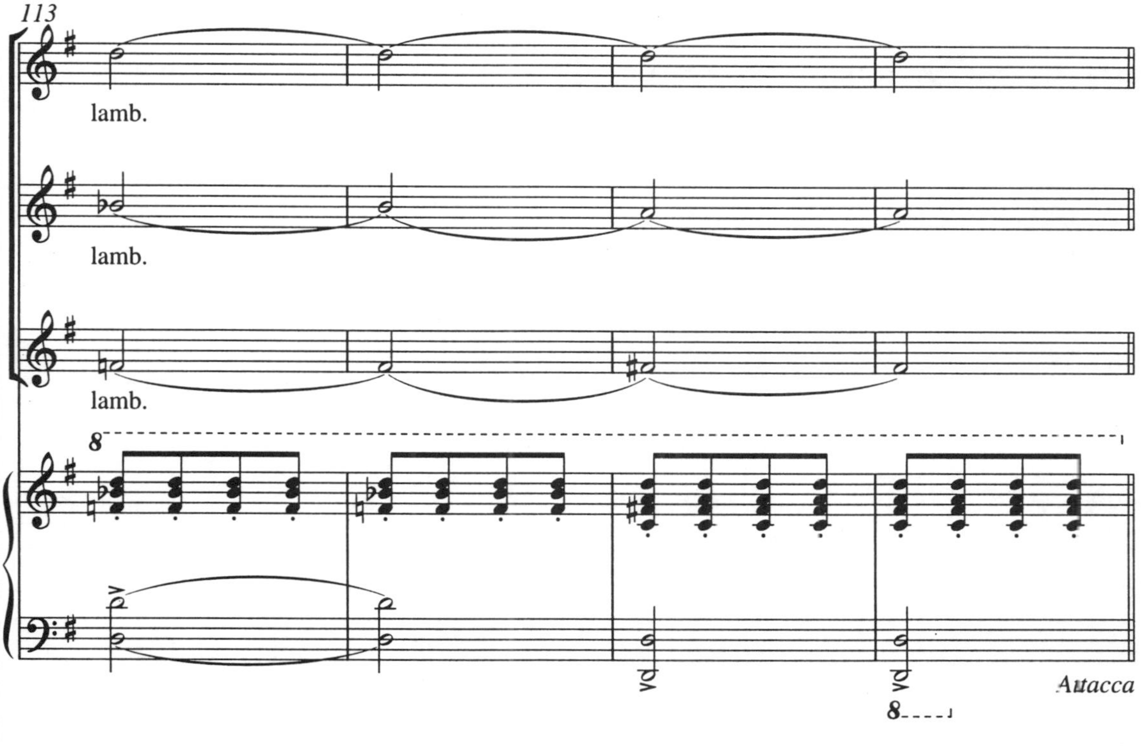
113
lamb.
lamb.
lamb.
8
Attacca
8

7. NATIVITY CAROL

Everybody sings this final section around the crib, individual characters and groups taking particular lines where appropriate.

13
Peace on earth, good - will to all' is the an - gels' song of joy.
Peace on earth, good - will to all' is the an - gels' song of joy.
17
All
Wel - come to the ba - by Je - sus, ly - ing on a bed of
8
pp
20
hay. Wel - come to the ba - by Je - sus.
8

23
Three Kings,
Shepherds and sheep
Wel - come, Christ - mas Day. Now at last our jour - ney's
loco
8
sub. pp
26
end - ed. Frank-in-cense and myrrh we bring.
8
29
All
Pre-sents for the ba - by Je - sus. Gold for the in - fant
8

32
Descant
Ah,
ah,
All
King.
Ah,
ah,
35
All
ah.
Look at the star shi-ning down on the sta - ble.
38
Look at the star shi-ning down where he lies.
Look at the star shi-ning down

41
on the sta - ble, light-ing up the Christ - mas skies.
44
1
2
Look at the star, look at the star.
Look at the star shi-ning down on the sta - ble. Look at the star shi-ning down
47
Look at the star,
where he lies. Look at the star shi-ning down on the sta - ble,

50
Descant
light-ing the skies.
'Glo - ria in ex -
All
light-ing up the Christ - mas skies.
'Glo - ria in ex -
53
cel - sis, praise the ba - by boy.
cel - sis De - o, praise the ba - by boy.
56
Peace on earth, good - will to all', is the an - gels' song of
Peace on earth, good - will to all', is the an - gels' song of

59
joy.
All
joy.
Ga - ther all a - round to wor - ship.
8
sub. pp
62
Ga - ther all a - round to pray.
Wel - com - ing the in - fant
8
65
Descant
Day.
Je - sus.
wel - come Christ - mas Day.
8
loco

69
Descant
'Glo - ria in ex - cel - sis, praise the ba - by boy.
All
'Glo - ria in ex - cel - sis De - o, praise the ba - by boy.
8
con Ped.
73
Peace on earth, good - will to all', is the an - gels' song of joy.
Peace on earth, good - will to all', is the an - gels' song of joy.
77
fff
'Glo - ria in ex - cel - sis, praise the ba - by boy.
fff
'Glo - ria in ex - cel - sis De - o, praise the ba - by boy.
8
fff

81
allargando
Peace on earth, good - will to all', is the an - gels'
Peace on earth, good - will to all', is the an - gels'
allargando

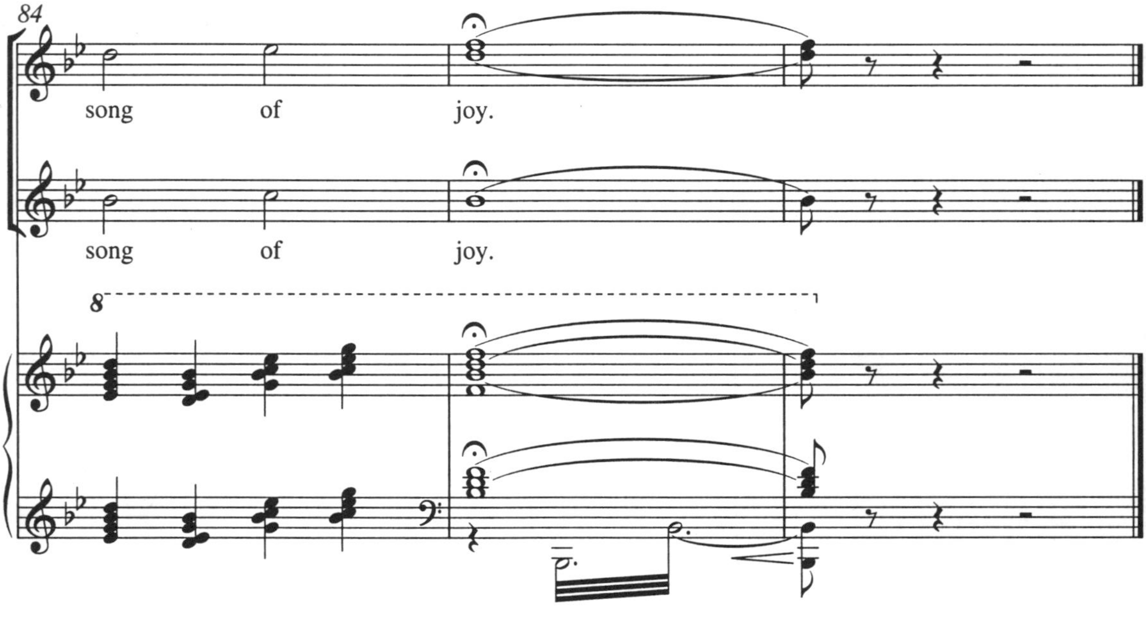
84
song of joy.
song of joy.
8